# Break on Through

New and Selected Poems, Volume 1

## Paul Nemser

LILY POETRY REVIEW BOOKS

Published by Lily Poetry Review Books
223 Winter Street
Whitman, MA 02382

https://lilypoetryreview.blog/

ISBN: 978-1-957755-08-3

Cover art: Lunar Landscape, ©Jesseca Ferguson, 2019, cyanotype

# Table of Contents

# PREFACE TO VOLUME I

*"You know the day destroys the night. Night divides the day. Tried to run. Tried to hide. Break on through to the other side."*

The sense of conflict, terror, and liberation in The Doors' song, "Break On Through (To The Other Side)," blew me away when I first heard it in 1967. If the Zeitgeist could speak, it would sound like that. I was seventeen, and I wanted to break away from childhood, high school, dependence, to break through the chains of repressive governments and the lies that had led to the Vietnam War. I wanted to break through the limits of ordinary language, which seemed wholly inadequate to capture that revolutionary moment in which all deadly limits could be overthrown, and we who had been in exile from the truth, the senses, our best selves, might find happiness, freedom, ecstasy, enlightenment. We might reclaim a bit of Eden. Poetry was the way.

That is why I chose "Break On Through" as the title of this first volume of Lily's two-volume *New And Selected Poems*. The selection includes three poems previously uncollected in books and an excerpt from my first poetry book, *Taurus*. All of these three are about trans-formation. Each poem describes an escape, a breakout, a breaking on through to the other side.

"Houdini" dates from 1972-1973. I was finishing up in Columbia University's M.F.A. program. Those were hard years for me, characterized by an undercurrent of paralysis and despair. My thesis adviser Stanley Kunitz quoted Rilke to me more than once: "You must change your life."

Instead of a final philosophy paper, I wrote a poem. It used the charac-ter of Harry Houdini, the escape artist and debunker of false magic, to talk about the dialectic between inner world and outer world, in which the self is constantly in motion, seeking transcendence. My Houdini embodied a system of concepts—similar to the characters in Blake's Prophetic Books, which my friend Mark Rudman and I were studying at the time.

In my exit conference at Columbia, I asked Kunitz what I should do next. I had no money. I had put myself through Columbia by working in a bookstore and taking out student loans. My parents had more or less disowned me for pursuing poetry, rather than something practical. And, as far as I know, no one graduating from the Columbia writing program in my year had yet found a college teaching job. When I told all this to Kunitz, he turned his large eyes to the ceiling and was silent for about a minute. Then he looked at me straight on and said, "The law."

I met my wife Rebecca in late 1973, and we married soon after, in 1974. Since we met, she has been the love of my life and the most important person in my life. She still is. Throughout those 48 years, she has believed in my poems—inspired them, read them closely, and commented on them with love, judgment, and skill.

We discovered early on that we had very different interpretations of events and expectations of the future. Rebecca focused on the positive, and I on the negative. She believed good things would happen, and I expected bad things to happen. Once, for example, we drove by a cake shop where several people were gathered outside. I said: "There must have been a robbery!" Simultaneously she said, "There's going to be a wedding!" My poem from the 1970's, "It Would Be Better," expresses my idea—and my growing love—of how she understood the world.

A few years after we married, I decided to follow Kunitz's advice and go into law. I began practicing law in 1980 at a large Boston firm (about 100 lawyers at the time). I had never worked high in a skyscraper, with long, quiet, internal corridors populated by suited lawyers on the outside, other employees on the inside, and an array of machines: typewriters, telephones, "Mag card" machines, telexes, faxes, copiers, and a mainframe primarily used for accounting. Once late at night when no one was around, I heard loud, rapid typing in a nearby office. I knocked on the door to introduce myself. No answer. When I opened the door, I saw only a desk with a telephone, a type-writer, and a thick black cable connecting them.

The experiences of those first years at the law firm seemed removed from human feeling and human life. Sometimes they made me think of Kafka or of Stanislaw Lem. Though my job demanded most of my attention and time, I soon began to write poems about it. This was the genesis of my long poem, "In the Beautiful City," which I worked on through most of the 1980's. During those years, I learned to enjoy aspects of working in the law—writing, argument, questioning, the intensity of a hard-fought contest, friendships, and travel to places I'd never been. More important, life changed in other ways: our son was born, my mother became fatally ill and died, things took on a differ-ent rhythm and a different meaning, My poem, accordingly, moves through alienation and grief toward love.

The longest section of this selected volume is an excerpt from my book *Taurus*. In 2005, I visited our son for a couple of weeks when he was studying in St. Petersburg, Russia. St. Petersburg was literary, exotic, threatening, and beautiful. I felt a connection with it. My ancestors came from Ukraine, Poland, and Lithuania—I grew up on borscht and blintzes—and my poetry had been influenced by Russian poets, especially Mandelstam, Pasternak, and Akhmatova. When my trip was over, I felt I had to go back. I applied to Summer Literary Seminars and returned to St. Petersburg in 2006.

Even more than the first trip, this visit made me feel the phantasma-gorical nature of the city. Ordinary laws— including those of physics and biology—no longer applied. Everything seemed possible. People behaved like statues, and statues like people. Bronze horsemen could come alive. The statue memorializing a nose who became man-sized and ran through the city was stolen from its niche. Rivers and canals cast kaleidoscopic light on the stage-set palaces near the water. Outside the apartment where Raskolnikov killed the old woman in Dostoyevsky's *Crime and Punishment,* fans wrote "Go Rodya!" in ink on the walls.

This formed the backdrop of my book *Taurus,* in which a bull-gargoyle in St. Petersburg is possessed by a god, comes down from the walls, walks the city, and falls in love with a mysterious woman named Europa. After I wrote it, I realized that *Taurus* was another poem about breaking through the deadening debris and coming alive

Years later I discovered a different connection to the Doors' song "Break On Through." Its music had been influenced heavily by Brazilian Bossa Nova and especially by *Getz/Gilberto,* my father's favorite record album, which I must have heard a thousand times in my teen years. Beginning in the late 1990's, I began making work trips to Brazil, met wonderful people there, explored parts of its endangered paradise, heard a lot of live music—Samba, Bossa Nova, Tropicália, Forró, and other styles. I had studied with Elizabeth Bishop at Harvard, and I found places in Brazil where she had lived. I learned enough Portuguese to read originals of poems that Bishop beautifully translated.

I lost myself and found myself again and again—in that Doors song, in Russia, and in Brazil; in the cold waters of Oregon, Massachusetts, and Maine; in love, in struggle, in grief, and in arguing the law; at the synagogue, the Seder, and prayers alone; in Genesis, Isaiah, Job, the Song of Songs; in the Tao Te Ching and t'ai chi chu'an; but most of all in moments of reading and writing poetry—as in *Taurus,* at the end of the long poem called "Ball Lightning": "Something bursts./ The god is here."

.

# Break on Through

# Houdini

Where the highway meets the thruway the concrete buckles
where the thigh grinds the calf the kneeknot balloons
where the speedway cuts north the shocks are thrown off balance
where the wrist snaps off a curveball the tendons break down
The plumber worms at the grimeway of the pipejoint
The janitor scrapes at the airway of the vent joint
The rabbi pries at the tree of life's arrnjoint
The student reads the lipjoints of his dead teacher's tome
There are joints in dark clouds when they labor to rain
Joints hinge the steamshovel hunkered in the dirt
There are joints in the tidal wave the sound wave the human wave
rolling breaking dissipating starwaves elbowing their way
      through the great jointed bowls

        \* \* \*

       They buried him

        in a straitjacket
        in an armored suit
        in a full-body
        plexiglass cast

        and he's broken out
        That's the story

        Harry Houdini
        spills from his coffin

        riding antbacks
        moldspores
        helixes of dust
        at armlevel

In out in out

Houdini the needle
stitches fabric
stretched
between movement
and rest

* * *

Houdini

chaotic unity
traveling with grace

the querulous swarm
of doublejoints flailing

his vacillations
fathering
subatomic riptides
gales of quarks

Charged stale air
surrounds Harry's hospital
whose specialist
bristles on our hands

a static electricity
inflaming

the hesitant arm at the holster
the businesslike hand in the bed
the father forgetting the name of his son
the nightwatchman snuffing a light

the referee barking Break Break
waving his arms for a TKO
the ape wired for pleasure for pain
yanking electrodes from his head

Houdini
Harry Houdini the leech

plucking out decisions like shrapnel
feeding through his needly proboscis

Harry Houdini the thief

bursting unashamed from a cashbox
sweeping the floor with his hamstrung body
slipping out of his skin into chains

Harry Houdini the justice

catching his robe in the movement of a watch
denying the motions of immobility
excusing the jury from the specious present
beating his gavel on the inertial frame

Harry Houdini the god

coming down in a cloud of indecision

Distinctions blur
Shockwaves set in
The day-curtain bellies out
Harry swarms in
The night-curtain bellies out

* * *

Houdini underground
you dug
reached a well

You were content
with space enough
for your nostrils

The tarpot
spigot shut off
oozes anyway

mars the fine
black meander
of a watererack

meticulously plugged

I closed the valve
can do no more

the tar pouring

\* \* \*

There's an earthmover
who doesn't stop moving

a water-mover
who doesn't stop breathing

fibrillator
motivator
anti-simpIisticator

carrying sacks
from gravity fields
up the elevators

falling
through the airholes
of fallow slugfarms

even as he climbs
through the nailholes
of molefarms

up toward a keyhole
in the pavement
of a road

\* \* \*

Harry hefting fertilizers
gram-erg coagulators

germinating seeds
trapped in
weightless suspensions

secreted by cold-breathing
jelly-jelly mascerators

gnawing the gunny sacks
covered with salt

by one Houdini
Harry Houdini

who throws his weight
around the shriveling
sackbiters

lassos cryogenic jaws
the protodragon sneeze

just as a wind
smokes our last cigarette
that we turn
in the lock of our
last cerebration

Harry hears us calling
for a simple solution

\* \* \*

Harry plans
his itinerary

down to
the slightest
contortion

He rows a tunnel
cut
according to
gravity's blueprint

Knees to chest
straightlegged
knees to chest

Ribbed
like a car's grill
his stomach
begins to cramp

He's driving

Latticeworks
of cities
unbuckle
unhinge
in his flexible hands

He's rowing driving
west east

cloverleafing
county lines
dismantled
even as he crosses

Harry
who explains us

traffic planner
charting us

Harry

who delineates
the thoroughfares

stakes out
the roadsigns
and locks

*To go in*
*you go out*
*Make a body*

*To go out*
*you go in*
*Break a body*

Each downward step
links with the step before

The lower he sinks
the warmer the ice
sheared like glass from my back

This much is true
This much

Harry I'm digging you out
digging you into the air

# It Would Be Better

*for Rebecca*

Sound of the pots, weather in the kitchen.
Outside the air was laced with mist,
and brothers hugged sisters

on the black concrete. In winter,
everything would be better.
It would be all better in the spring.

An ounce of brandy and a cake
would decorate the table.
A bit of meat would steam like summer.

Teacups would not stain
when they went to drink.
There would be sex and oaken tables,

tools of good steel, a day's pay, and rain
washing the linens. Children
would not hide from passersby.

The grocer would hand out celery
to the thirsty. Cats would mop sweat
off a washerwoman's legs

while the wise sent incantations
to blue the heavy sky. Even politicians, learning
lines of old songs, would serenade them

of all that was to be. They might have a car.
And husbands and wives. They might learn
to play cello. They might weep.

So masons stirred and  stirred their mortar.
In the rich man's courtyard,
a gardener prayed for sun.

Nothing could contain their happiness.
Here was a beetle, beetles rolled
dung, dung grew wheat, wheat was history,

wave upon wave of famine and flood
to drive out the worst, knit the better
minute to minute into forever,

as clarinets might weave
night-thoughts of lovers,
whose ears would always hold the tune.

When light came down
like a tent over the workshops,
people bent over wheels

looked up from their jobs, saw
each other's faces, called out what needs fixing
by hammer or by thread. by hand or by flame.

In open-windowed rooms,  they traded
forgivenesses,  contexts, distinctions
till night healed to day.

Some had been bumpkins, and some had been lucky,
and if buildings got too tall
for people to handle, gulls that wheeled

like machines of salvation
would teach them directions
from the flock's own map.

Signs would arrow off the freeway.
The roads would not be crowded.
There would be messages. and long times,

doorways, joy, and mourning.
It would be sweet and good
because so much had gone before.

# In The Beautiful City

1.
I kept pulling levers
so as not to lose connection,
the hook-up to the larger organon,
and was amazed at the sheer

inhumanity of the motion,
repeated till numb I felt
the pull of the river,
the pleasant, unanswerable desire

to be other; as things
in human guise resemble us,
beckoning like the souls of lovers.
Was that your voice?  you said.

And I:  was that you?
And loudspeakers played tunes
that swept us along,
our movements ever more instinctual.

Let me begin how the wind brought fever,
and I heard a heart
in the air compressor.
Had I seen that light before

on the waves, on the shore,
in the quicksilver splash
of an albacore
hooked, slashed, pressed into cans?

Light cut me off
in the midst of movement.
Everyone was on a video screen,
deep in reminiscences of human action,

welcoming, retreating,
like dear ones in a dream,
but even there, water was moving.
Even stillness

moved through the flux,
crossing a forehead,
shiver on a shoulder,
in the factory where I heard a heart,

and the great derrick
turned on its axis
under clouds professing thunder
rippling the vats.

Grapples turned their hooks toward heaven.
For all I knew, it could have been earth.
I too was moving,
molten as the steel.


2.
Under factory floodlights, the conveyors
bent like a stream
thrust deep into land, then back
oceanward, the black glide

through banks of shouting people;
widening, the wave
expired in the gasp of sprayguns;
leviathan's motors revved up

to rip the sod of a mechanized field
where even oats were trademarked
to the protein.  Nothing
was too small.

Earth had become a small place,
a fleck in time, a flit in space,
a byte, a wave, a valuable trace
of seasalt and useful ore.

Business took place
at the intersections
of light-speed currents,
and connections.

Out of the tiny, endless change.
Out of the dwindling, the new.
On behalf of a few corporations,
the sun was rising through the sulphur.

Buildings were rising, yellow-windowed,
like slow-growing crops.
Goods passed in procession
beyond the reach of any retina

down hazy, jazzy canyons
where sky meets the street
through warehouses into orbit
across lakes and into bodies

from keystrokes into TVs
and winding and winding.
Belts spanning the country
drove minds drowsy in the crossing

or simply carried them off
like pigs newly slain
in great pink piles of eternal peace
never having looked so gentle.

Rich ones, poor ones,
middling shivering pure ones
shook from the static
in their telecommunications

on the jostling banks
where they jockeyed for position
to receive new deliverables, never quite usable,
in definitive, but alterable designs.

Listen! The thirsting
and the amphitheatrical hush.
There, in the waters,
was a half-human head

announcing the newest representation
among delegates of the material persuasion
who spoke in eerie unison,
eyeless and orphaned,

"What do you see
when you peel the onion?"
"I see a landscape
incapable of tears."


3.
With claws in water, a sphinx-like expression,
I fished for a semblance
to approximate the past:
love sundered, joined,

like running water sundered,
and the wind seemed to shake me from inside.
I thought of the sound
of my mother breathing

and repeated riddles
to whatever I encountered.
Was love the last thing memory wanted?
Was the last thing the first thing was love?

Thinking of answers increased my fever.
Surrounded for miles,
I saw only the river.
Rush of goods, information,

products, prices, tangling like eels
in unfeeling interinanimation
through the waters of the factory
so swift and sleepy

in the throes of a civilizing transformation.
Violence was the synonym.
Violence the antonym.
I was a man.  Grown.

A social creation, adrift
in the hot oblivious waters.
First man, first child, first born.
Raised up to see from a great prospect

the changeless interchange, death and dream,
in the work I was doing--
was it work for the waking? --
the work I was born to in the world.


4.
From nothing but a silicon
waist curving narrow,
and hips hopelessly
hopelessly wide, in the glass,

the clear uterus of time,
where the sand of his seconds
met the sand of her hours,
and the flow of the sand,

the heartbeat of the sand,
belly and penis and soul of the sand,
the child of the sand-- that was I,
late the king of digits,

of dials and constellations,
key meeting fingertip,
seed of the future.  O river,
may you never run dry!


5.
I kept seeing obstacles
in every description.
Could it be the unpronounceable
was shaping the air

and the stammering daybreak
fled his arrows,
the broken heartbeat
washed on shore

as the sun looked in
behind the door,
and found the knot
in the mire and rot

that held shadows to the floor:
horse, horseman,
dreamer, dream,
stepping through the muddy stream,

dumpsite, ass-end, smokestack, outfall,
licking the lead in a cubicle wall;
sun behind the news, a data eclipse,
blotting the views

of roses' hips,
or birds'claws, or a squirrel's fall
or microchips
that decode a call?

To me corruption
was the narrowing of vision.
And destiny --
a bomb in transition.

Everywhere glass and glass on fire.
Blind eyes blinking over a pyre.
When I looked,
I too could not see.


6.
Not used to lunch hours,
man hours, sunless time,
I haunted the city of many markets,
still young and lost and looking.

Windowshopping, what had I become?
The lure of goods was rebranding the river.
Had I lost all feeling?  Did I cross over?
Forever, it seemed, in the bottomless glass,

I watched a creature of efficiencies
aflush with odds and angles
feeling tall as heaven with economies of scale.
Buy! said my eye, and the goods passed.

I paid cash.  Ignored people.
At the bank, punched my number.
The machine asked what transaction I wanted.
Then I knew: I wanted bliss.


7.
I saw the sinuous passage before me,
heard my mother's voice.
"Dus vet zayn dayn baruf."
Raisins and almonds.

Ineluctable current.
Through the giant cablework
electrons flew,
and I knew at that moment

she would not save me.
The time was mine to change
or yield to.  There was only
one design.  It was then

my loneliness came to me,
compressing my heart.
And in the cacophonies
of metal, I felt

the meekness of machines.
They were kind as pigs,
but they ate no corn.
Predictable and temperate,

they did not reproduce.
They transmitted by the telephone.
They were the telephone!
And O the way they talked to me

on visual read-out!
How my breath caught
near the high-speed printer!
The look of the console

as I programmed it solo,
and it told me the square root of two.
You were saying something to me
about needing a lover

and how in sympathy
we would see forever,
and how we could never compute the number
of times we could return.


8.
O, you said.  O what, and I was dreaming,
was floating on waters,
caught a glimpse, had a feeling.
The water smelled salty,

and the sky was clearing.
Even the smoke above the beautiful city
had a way of looking like writing,
and the stars had the look of a sea.

A sign lit up across the cloud—
it said splendor—and water broke open
twelve doors round the center,
and all the stories

told to the ocean
were untold in whitecaps,
unrolled in rips,
unrelenting in the bow of a back;

wet, wet, in the curve
as they found you, and
you were turning
over in the sand.


9.
And I turned to you,
for the last thing, the first thing.
Earth Angel, Earth Angel,
the Penguins sang,

as if from the polar star.
Had there ever been such looking
and navigations?  Ever such finding
and what elation!

I saw every latitude in a drop of water.
Lakes stretched
to the farthest round of the planet,
and trees serrated s

hillside and pit.
An avalanche of whales
splashed into the river
making a wave

that overwhelmed
all remnants of structure.
Even to the end of things.
Even to the center.

For a time I laughed like a gander,
and all we said
had hilarious clarity.
For a time we knew nothing,

only rolled and rolled
down dunes till we smashed
our fresh water into sea
and woke somewhere foreign

under the sun, free
as if the galaxies conversed
along our arteries,
Now and Now and Now.


10.
Blue waves crisscrossed
beside the factory island.
Your eyes fixed mine, began
to widen.  The wind was cool.

You looked like a blossom
opening in slow, generous motion.
Larksong in the deep
back-flowing sand.

I saw memory more clearly
than what I saw.
And the memory
that transfixed me

was alive in a future
conjured from Edens,
ages of gold, painted murals
on the handles of plows.

Mountain mist, hillsides
of peasants, ships at a city
in crooks of valleys.
Hands doing, lips clucking,

cows' macerations;
winged arms fall into sea
and no one looking.
But O that feeling

when he rose so high
and what repose when he
crashed to the bottom
crossed the preoccupied face

of the plowman
whose life continued its own
directions
to and fro along the side

of the mountain
in the gorge where miracles
always happened.
Angels thrummed, the messiah

came, and centaurs
shook their manes at a stranger,
pranced clip clop
by the weeping water

that searched the catacombs
and cleansed the traveler,
for there was no
unkindness in it,

though it hunted its lover,
and above ground
time ran back and forward
simultaneously toward eternity.

11.
There are cities where my heart
has poured its best
into the fountains,
and I've been borne up

as if I'd found my destination
in a word or the deepening
of an eye.  You turned to me,
and love was in the rotation.

I found your glance,
The hill was green with cultivation.
Grapes in baskets,
plums in the hand,

mushrooms with an odor
of the richnesses of earth.
An embrace by a well,
the clear, clear water.

The sun was going down,
but the moon was rising.
Your left hand touched my right;
soon the other two

were meeting, and before sleep
we saw a new planet rising
through choked calls,
the multiplying halls

of gas rending, spirits split
past rescue or grace,
but here the wind was a womb
for our soarings,

and the house we were making--
others might come too:
children, old friends
ancestors, citizens;

mammals in garden burrows,
songbirds in their seasons;
wildflowers, thistle seeds,
raspberry, salmon,

goddesses with gray eyes, flute-playing gods,
harps and sarods and balalaikas,
dragons and swordsmen, elephants and emus,
taoist masters and divining rods,

roses climbing the trellis of the gateway,
and a galaxy, and a ladder of light,
reaching to the pinnacle of night.
A city, rivers, a sea.

from TAURUS

# Foreword

A few years into the millenium, I was staying in a hotel in St. Petersburg, a converted apartment just off of Nevsky Prospekt. Mine was one of several small, steamy rooms around a shared bath. Each room had a single, springless bed and a tiny desk.

It was almost the summer solstice--white nights--and after tossing and turning in the light, I went down to the breakfast room for kasha and a hard boiled egg. When I got back upstairs, I noticed that the door to a room near mine was wide open. The room looked as if it had been abandoned in haste.

Strewn on the floor were heaps of papers with Cyrillic writing, some typed, some in a hard, jagged hand. I started gathering these papers up, I'm not sure why. Since I didn't know Russian, I took some pages down to the desk clerk.

Shaking his head and shrugging, he translated slashes of handwriting: "Have city. Have bull. Bouncer--Rock Club Winter. Robot arms? What is this? Arms in love. Russian brides, radium watch dials. These are sold. Have movies, matryoshkas, personals. Borealis. Ball lightning. . . . Ok. Ok. Is good. A bull-gargoyle. Comes to life. Sometimes a god possesses him. A model. Mysterious. Name: Europa. Bull meets girl, and all Hell breaks loose."

# Europa's crossing

**She dreams a meeting.**  When I try to cross a border,
the moon is full.

I listen for footsteps.
Do they come for me?

I listen for eagles.
Have I reached the sea?

Antelope rivers
bound away into the firs.

Is that you, my bull,
crashing through tall stalks, my guide?

The clouds go fast.
Full moon, moonspray, no moon.

My fate steps forelegs
down out of the sky.  My exile

beckons with shaken horns.
My husband bears me on his back

toward crosshatch birches,
where gods and men

walk in the same shadows—
walk with the raven and the wolf—

over snow cracks
of a dark imperium.

## Taurus waking

**He returns to life**   Not far from Fontanka down a steam-hazed pinch
at a hidden turn in a little-walked street
in a building stranded in breathless depths,

once the home of a minor prince,
then apartments for titanium workers,
now a cavern—offices and shops—

behind a green façade that sprinkles plaster
when the summer moon
slices night like beets into concentric rounds.

That's when old women shout to keep cool,
and gargoyles—animal, bird, and every mix—
sleep in their niches, Taurus among them,

at peace, until the god is with him,
and metal softens, brackets give,
horns and fingers start to move.

His seized joints echo against the walls.
His first steps fail. He crawls into the light,
a metal man in the costume of a bull

hoisting himself up to his full height.
Hooves hit like iron on an empty street.
The city swirls, nightblind.

through museums for every kind.
Rain's erupting.  He's had nothing to eat.
No idea what his heart may want of him tonight.

## Ice cream

**The bull-gargoyle.
watches a vendor
in a park.**

Look at the vendor's footsore, forward lean
to scrape a tub of *Keep in Shape Energy Ice Cream*
before an audience of squirrels.

Every hour he scoops.  Squirrels dive after drips.
And neither they nor any bull can say what customers recall—
whatever streams, is wasted, sold,

skimmed, scummed, balls of sweetest bean or fruit.
Nothing outlives the moment it's seen.  And seen,
and seen again.  So the stars know

light's endless return as it comes around the curves,
nothing lost, just forever changed.
The bull watching, drowsily,

as the scoop forms layer upon layer.
Cow milk lipids, free and bound, speak directly to his nose,
like a thickened cloud of kisses.

For seconds he loses the direction of time
as if the ball were forming in some rural back
when his foremost thought was grass and mother,

mother and grass and a blackbird.
And in that same scoop, he spots the flower of what's to be,
a tune he thinks he knows, or will,

or once lowed in giant amorous bursts
to tangled, tender female wisps,
beauty out of cloud, the looking eye glommed

31

on a knee, white as an ice cream cone,
till all focus came apart,
and he could not say what he had seen.

Lightning's afterimage bleaches us blind, so we grasp
at stray scraps, a sprinkle, a fold, as if gods'
fortunes could be known, or animals' could be told.

Thus, a bull's fate is written on a match snapped afire,
phosphorus-hot, ephemeral desire
that cones up a ball of cloud

in the street where he was going, the milky street.
A body he's been, but there's a wring to his hump,
neck twisted back to see what's coming.

# The sighting

**Looking up from his soup, Taurus sees a rotating billboard, his first view of Europa**

Bull-gargoyle over a bowl of borscht
forgets for a moment that teetering existence
on a baroque roof, that uncomfortable

crouch, fixed, about to jump,
He pauses like one of those museum escapees—
actors, in period dress,

who pose for photos for a few rubles.
Their odd way of standing for hours, theatrical
    and pallid.
Their antique hats and collars

that frame the points and hollows of the skull.
But he's a god in the costume of a gargoyle
in a speed-shocked age,

antennae in his horns, mirror glasses.
He reads Roman letters from a scrolling placard—
photos of a model, her thick, open lips.

How palpable she is across land and water,
her dusky electricity
almost in his metal reach.

Synapses idling, he peers down into his soup
as if an undiscovered
dimension were curled up in the bowl.

# Europa

**The bull-gargoyle thinks about a model he has just seen on a rotating billboard.**

Mind drifts to the placard's
beautiful rotation.
Even still,

she moves freely,
in fire.
She dances older newer

than the stars in Winter's cages.
Was anyone
ever so free to appear?

Her eyes humorous,
her forehead naïve,
as if she's

read
and forgotten
everything.

# Dream over dream

**The bull-gargoyle, in St. Petersburg, imagines that Europa dreams she too is there; a boat ride.**

Walking by Fontanka, I imagine you dreaming
that I see you dreaming on an evergreen bed,
and so we are together. It's night where you sleep.

Long past moonset, I rise behind mountains.
I climb them to look at you, fitful in bed.
You wonder at the brightness—only linked stars?

Nearly waking, but sleep ripples over.
A boat glides up with songs and flags.
Here is Fontanka. Here are the banks.

We board, haze-blind. The sinuous canal
wiggles vodka out of bottles, ghost boats in a dance.
At the back of the queue, ours pitches and rocks.

We duck heads under bridges, and fireworks explode.
I see nothing, love, nothing—infinite, daring,
your eyes, gray-green, the waters in them.

# To the stockyard bulls

The bull-gargoyle
addresses the bronze
bulls who once stood
by the gates of
the old stockyard
in St. Petersburg.

My bronze brothers, they cut exactly where our hearts were.
They knew us in the chutes and bellowing on blocks,

in wrapped paper parcels tinged with blood—
handed to women in chicken-print kerchiefs—

chewed in grand style by brush-bearded men in crimson vests
and long coats, who crumpled into chairs after dancing.

And here you are—tilt-headed, nostrils huge,
tensed to leap when there is no need to run,

having outlived the slaughterers and their house,
their long-tongued hounds lapping offal.

Trailered to the peeled pink gates of a former meat plant,
your bronze is more solid than the stage-set columns,

your legs more stout than the truck tires
heaped in squat, white-pink garages.  Don't despair, brothers,

the gods ignite any and all.  Some who leave streaks
like window water, others pent up in monumental pause.

They enjoy sitting inside us, ribbed bronze for a chassis.
In cool belly hollows, you'll feel a stirring

just as grass begins to push through gravel,
though your ears cradle gray-feather snow.

# Her image—Griboedov Canal

**The bull-gargoyle,
tormented by images of
the model Europa.**

It drives me mad—
these executions
of curve and tone.

I envy the photographers
who saw you live:
golden airy thinness,

a direct unceasing gaze
as if the lens had a soul.
But I see simulacra.

Colonies of starlings
flit and loop before me—.
you on billboards, you on-screen.

Your language!
I sit at Кофе Хауз, coffee house,
near Gryphon Bridge,

on the phone, Телефон.
Molecules of coffee almost
glow up like embers in the stifled air.

I order "espresso."
I watch the scene.
Flying lions draped

with languorous lovers.
Snapshot. Snap. No haze, no shade.
Snap. Snap. Every shot rips a hole.

Is it like that for you,
my photogenic bird?
Lightbringer, when the shutter closes.

# A bus goes by

**The bull-gargoyle
sends a song to
Europa; her image
on passing buses.**

Exposed at a flood-barrier building site,
the bog, choked with pylon and wall,
is patrolled by gulls and feral cats.
One summer dusk, I bring fishheads for all,

and a bus goes by.  There you are on a phone,
in a striped T-shirt behind chrome bars.
Your geisha wince, as if sun never reached you.
"Locked in?  No network?  We'll give you ears!"

A thin-lipped man drinks vodka, peppered.
Three cats trail as I swerve between cars.
The man's empty bottle shatters near them,
outbursts of eye-cutting ice and stars.

Hydrocarbons overflow like milk
through the canals and past the park
where bear dancers whirl like holy fools
around a cub through the never-dark.

A bus goes by, and I'm anxious as a calf.
Now, in the shock of sun, I send you text
in the presence of the grid, in the presence of a god.
feeling your presence and the next

bus blowing by.  Are you spirit, then?
Deep as a plunge off a sacred hill,
heart in flame like fire seen through rain—
so pale in brightness; in movement, so still—

or are you explosions of sycamores,
a circus contortionist's dance on her head,
the calendar's windows open to sea,
lanterns passing through homes of the dead,

an owl, barred by branches and moon
from flying to me, though I hear you call,
though you call all night, from far away
into my orifices, into my cell.

Waiting can't fill us.  The build never stops.
Rubs of light unravel my eye.
Canals and terns.  Headlonging love.
My coat drips  A bus!  A bus goes by.

# Attachment:  Virtual Matryoschka

**An email attachment
in which the bull-
gargoyle imagines
Europa as a nesting
matryoschka doll.**

There are as many foreign objects
on earth as in the sky,
a paradoxical finding.

All these divisions—
space into time chambers,
time into space!

And I have come to see perfection
in all forms is divisible,
high or low, deity or dust mote,

even you,
my perfect many-in-one,
and so I have had made

this matryoschka of you,
of captured impulses
and sparks.

You inside you
and inside that
is you,

child-sized you, fingernail you,
the tiniest speck
without flaw.

# Stroll

**Taurus the bull-gargoyle, inhabited by a god and Yevgeny the robot arm take a walk.**

Never been a morning like this," says Taurus.
"There's never been this morning," says Yevgeny,
"Many are like, one identical,"

reading from his instruction set, which does the thinking.
Taurus has no instruction set. Only the god.
The god commands. Taurus does.

The god instructs. Taurus fights, learns.
His bronze legs creak like birds in their hip housings.
Corroding, Taurus is unlike the god

who moves morning to morning in a streak of bronze,
bull-fast, puffing and procreating.
This morning the god calls himself "Taurus." He says:

"Never been a morning so swift or so new—
now red-sun pools are steaming,
and mushrooms are learning to eat metal."

Taurus and Yevgeny stroll under morning firs,
bronze bull, robot arm squishing spongy ground,
the fungus under all.

## from *The Scrapbook Of Yevgeny The Robot Arm*

**The robot arm's
first scrapbook entry**

### Yevgeny's Birthday Address

O the energic mechanisms, my friends,
the rivet and the joint!
All is fixed, but has a pivot.

I cannot speak to you
but in the language you've given me.
And therefore on my birthday

as on the dawning day of "dawn" and "day,"
your interface faces mine
when I turn toward you,

and with a wave of my very arm,
I blow out beeswax candles
manufactured on visits to how many roses,

each one waving stem—an arm,
blossom—a hand,
each one having said, as I do—I am.

### Yevgeny's reach

**The robot arm's
credo**

Maintain a small footprint, citizens,
a small footprint.
Be small where you anchor.
From there, unfold.

Like arms of the wind, reach through branches
to shake the petioles
at the orange brink.

Every stretch has a starting point.
Every mound is a mountain.
Before the world was matter, a ray stood up.

Up—and then it moved.


## Chips by night

**The robot-arm's chips meditate, activate; his eye.** It's the cobalt hour when waves
float like stitches through phosphorescence.

Sparks, once born, die faster
than we can catch them in our nets.

Moon's hand ladles the sea into a bay.
Wind's hand spatters it out as spray.
A comb of stars parts the dark.

We're alive as kelp or krill, though we're alloy and resin,
silicon, copper, acid, flame.
In our caves of sand, currents flow and knit.

An eye sees the lab. The eye of Yevgeny
sees a square of moonlight pour through like seawater,
over the still hand.


## Hand

Hand the Creator made all out of nothing,
**The robot-arm's chips creation myth** pushed back the night a fraction of a whir,
made owl out of— mesh out of—man out of –nothing,

where they'd sloshed in formless dislocations.
Hand lifted them out of the darkling womb.
They were butter sopping from a churn.

Hand the Creator had a hand with a hand,
in all an infinite adding of hands.
They assembled the world in no time. . .

Out of beaks and night's hair, mouse necks and rain,
crows' windless ambushes, gnats' cloudy massings,
miracle of who-ing in the mesh of night,

out of whom, says the man, says who, says the owl,
I, signs Hand, pointing like a beak
punching rows and columns of stars.

### Parable of the components

**The god of the robot arms conceives their components as birds.**

Hand the Creator wove birds upon birds,
And thus there were always wings in the air,
there was always nesting and feeding.
Here was a bird, landing in a birch.
There another bird hymned on a branch.
Hand scooped up songs that came off the branch
and wove them into birds upon birds.

### Yevgeny's paradox

**The robot arm takes his first breath**

The best rule is known from what follows,
best forgotten in what follows.
A rule's desire is best known in violation.

I am a robot arm. I cannot breathe.
My Ruler: "Yevgeny, do not breathe."
And I breathe. In terror of suffocation.

### A letter in another hand

The robot arm has
saved a letter from
his beloved, another
robot arm; here is
the letter.

I can't stop sighing.  My compressor's never full.
I'm a binary being in a bliss of rules!
The humans are sympathetic.  Kindly mouths
deform across their mandibles like honey down a wall.
But they give me green feathers and an alligator glove
when I crave algorithms, oil, and lightning.
We, my love, are in sequence, in phase—
ting and ping, the thunk of purpose.
White herons' long-legged mazurkas through mallows.

### Yevgeny's daydream

His reverie:
the biosphere.

The grace of wheat grains broken from a stalk.
I have no need of these, yet I love them.
Rain would set me sparking and shorting,
but I rejoice in its irregular tap.
Husks, toenails, lost mitochondria
soften in a stream among salmon skin and milt.
Pathos of a softer world.

### Yevgeny's homesickness

The robot arm, who
came from Tomsk
and now works in a
St. Petersburg lab,
contemplates
a carcass.

The dead winter squirrel in the driveway;
by summer a fluff-puff gray tail.

The forepaws, taken up by a tire,
now spin through Siberia.

Drop an acorn by my home, little hands.
Drop an acorn there for me.

### Yevgeny's letter to Lyuba

**The robot arm answers his beloved.**

You've undone me.
I have given up the Eden
in my gears' mindless meshing.

### Yevgeny thinks of insects

**The robot arm's affinity for insects**

I have learned to play instruments
without tapping a foot
Action's best confined to needed motion, as a seawind
brings only the necessary squall—
big enough to sprout a lettuce seed.
An ancient voice locked in a human voicebox
calls to me in songs of grinding stone.
Scratches and quakes! I can barely understand.
The garden is green because
the infrastructure has not reached it.
Today, more cricket than man,
I long to walk in dirt
and macerate a rootling,
to lock on a mate and make larvae, every second to an end
unfogged by many selves,
to be gathered around a single, small "i."
I am an arm. Armness enlivens me.
Is it so much better to be glorious,
chasing grand uses in the feral twilight?
You humans walk eyes half-closed into night,
feeling for a tingle, a respite.
There's less air each time you breathe in.
My six-legged soul wouldn't bend a grass blade.
Through my carapace
I'd bathe in little winds.

**Yevgeny's praxis**

**A call to arms**     Do not be eager.  Do not be slack.
There's no way without work.

This room's a desert.
Pack along, bounce over a rut.

Moments are meteors.  Look:
A finger streaks the dark!

**Yevgeny's faith**

There is permanence in repair.

# Phases

**The bull-gargoyle
thinks of Europa
as having different
phases, like water or
the moon.**

She is the fall wave that fetches boats up
on the Peterhof beach
when gulls hunt herring, rococo fountains loop,

and the princesses' peasant palaces
are feverish for glints
against the scalloped fish-gray of the bay.

She's a gated garden bordering a "Greek" temple's
gray, scalloped pools.
She's the white bubbles where water returns

from its airy arcs and cataracts
till fall collapses, vibration slows.
She's a groan on a darkening road of bones.

A railroad arrows the steppe in the throat.
Hands that stanch the bleeding
shrink to sticks, freeze as hooks.

She's the delicate bones in a broken foot
that walks and walks as ice collects ice,
numbing it, numbing it.

She barely leaves a print, yet she's liquefying there
as earth opens.  Borders change.
She is watercolor sinking into paper.

She drips beyond the edges, the drips now a stream,
stream's a torrent, the torrent dives.
She curls into chambers, hissing on magma.

A vision of Europa as the soul of magma.
Taurus has never witnessed such excitement
silhouetted in steam.

## Scarlet sails

When there is no night, the night crawlers

burrow even deeper
in the seepy loam.

When there is no night, the old looms

clacker at the new ones;
and silk falls like a river.

When there is no night, I look for you.

I find scarlet sails,
the slippery decks.

We cannot—almost—almost drink—all night amid

the fireworks' chatter, saying

free will's inescapable, and night is love's victim

(under halos of white birds and sodium lamps,
under brightening empires of slash and strike,

daffodils igniting in stratus.
O how much we drank!).

Sleep has no future when there is no night,

though bridges pass above us,
a brief gift and grief of night,

the hull a tympany irregular as hearts,

49

while spidery boats throw their silks upon the waters,
and the waters
wear them as night.

Touch this coppery skin, love.  It is the skin
of the broken, of regiments
corroding in snow.  Skin
of the saw's teeth, cutting as it saves.

Though I sink like the sun into a stand of pines,
though you turn to leather and I to sea,
be my sand, be my salt, be the shaking

that knew me
when there was no night.

# Europa declaims

**Europa anticipates
what she might
say upon meeting
the bull.**

I'll play any part.  I'll be a shovel.
I'll spread manure on banquet platters
and smear your temples' pitted steps.

Murderers may sleep soundly beside me,
but I'll dig up their wine-rich hillsides.
I, who can't be gripped or thrown away

will beguile with paradox.
Like this:  the terrible is never new.
To be terrible, it must have known us

when we trotted four-legged.
When I meet you, my terror, I shall know you.
I am an actress.  You are a bull.

Let that define us.  I'll be a cow.  You are a god.
If you do not want beef,
then milk me for bone.

If you do not want my milk,
I will calve for you,
and our children will pillage and plow

by the Aegean, by the windy cliffsides
of Apennine and Caucasus.
We shall teach them not to eat their own kind.

# Europa's monologue

### 1. An icon of the encounter

**She imagines what it will be like to think back on meeting the bull.**

Every breath is danger.
The bellows says *I know. I know. I know.*
One morning, the sun's a tangerine, the next
black bread ballooning.

Stickiness of memory, an icon's tempera,
animal glue and honey on alder.

I knew you once. I was bark-hard then.
Just born of seed, and branching.

That is when gods come to us
dressed in hide or wings.
Their beaks pinch foreheads.
Their hooves X our sex.

You were horns, or a memory of horns.
I prayed to your blackness.
It could have been whiteness.
Like every clarity that comes from god.

Like every past where gods are ambered
in animal glue and sap.

### 2. Time's directions

This is the reason all planes fly backward:
In other times, bulls were not simply bulls
to be studied on scientific principles.

Girl and bull and the dizzy moon,
a pasture's lavender smithereened.
Drunken temples, cartwheels in torchlight,
Ring-dance of girls, alder-green. . .

Now in casinos, I roll and roll.
Every tick risks a future.
Every outbreath's a kiss.

And I lose the make-up on my mask, find
blubber and bone.

This is why everyone
falls off:

My mother on the carousel horse at the front.
My mother on the carousel horse at the back.
A barebacking Cossack rides the roulette wheel.

This is the reason
all planes fly forward.
*I know. I know, know, know,* says the bellows,
when all it thinks, all it knows,
will be fire.

# The gargoyle's entreaty

**The bull-gargoyle resorts to formal argument entreating Europa to accept his love.**

Oblivious to the hearth
of this aging icy world
where all that moves is death,
I slumbered in fire's mold.
I hardened in a shape.
Tongs yanked me from the mold.
They dropped me near a pipe.
For months I slept in ash.
My only dream was sleep.
Ash came off with a brush.
A file scrubbed off my burrs.
A ballpeen was my lash.
I was the sum of scars.
I was a clapper's crash
for gods and revelers.
Function hammers form.
I stand upon a roof
and witness.  There's a swarm
of human bees, a cough
of little fates.  A worm
spins out a perfect life,
ennobles to a saint.
He's eaten for a laugh.
Half of all deeds are lint.
Half of all hopes are spoils.
One tries to wash.  One can't.
Loose love pours balms and oils.
Love is the end of one.
Love is for gods and fools,
for wire-borne girls, alone,
for sack-borne sperm that crawl
till genes' extinction,
or even for a bull
occasionally alive

when god delivers all
and unities revive
as body, mind, and soul.
This is the laugh of love:
It starts down in a bell.
It starts down in a shoe
and rises in a wail.
It lavas in the blue.
It heaves a trembling tail.
And then one dies in two,
and two may fuse in all,
for god makes one anew.
Then be with me and roll.
Let my blood play in you.
Sweet myrtle's pressings heal.
There's nothing death can do.

# Then Come

### 1.  The bull's humility

**A seduction**

A dust-scorpion runs from hiding, but my hoof beheads it.
I put the spiked tail in a tumbler of vodka, and we drink.
To the limitless gods who have graced us with defenses!
But you've no need to fend me off with hand or tongue.
I lower to the steppe, smitten—onto your petals, your pyre.

### 2.  Meeting

**The bull-gargoyle tells Europa how to find him.**

Were you left behind when everybody fled the last century?
Remember how you planned at the age of 6 to be a planner,
  to serve
and report, report and serve, with all the clean elegance of a
  gate that locks?
You still know the way to that gate, without directions
  or footprints.
You know it like fresh air and foam, like dill and black pepper.
Just as I found it one day in the labyrinth,
and parted your latch as if you were the monster.
You before you knew it was you.  Look for me there.

### 3.  Knees

**The bull-gargoyle speaks of her desire.**

Look there.  In that fire.
In the blue

that curls and spits in the alderwood,
you see horns.

You see haunches
formed in the spicy smoke.

How then do I stand on the beach before you,
a bull, solid and white?

On white-hot hoofs that boil
the salt flood wetting your knees.

### 4.      Knowing

**The bull-gargoyle tells Europa that being with him will bring her knowledge.**

I will speak to you of things known only to the god.
How do I know them?  Because he is with me.
How remember?  He does not strike them from my mind.
Why am I not soundless, like a bell his hand has quelled?
There is a girl, sincere as a siltless creek,
generous as a hot spring shallows,
the shape of a goddess god-made for passion
like a mix of clay and glass red-heated on Olympus
and motorcycled to this room by the Winter Palace,
a back room in what was once a stable,
there to cool perfect as a shadow of a pear,
to ripen in the darkness that swells in these walls.
The secrets I will tell her, the ways she will give in,
as we glide ever deeper, room by room,
and every key I show will tell all about its keyhole.
All of her doors and all the spaces
will know the mercies of the many-fingered god.

# Visitation

**Europa's dream**

I hear a wave, angular and wet.
*Only one wave.*

It is a sea, though I sleep in mountains.
*One come alive.*

How did he come here, the one I awaited?
*Changing rain.*

Bull, my only, other-than-earthly—
*Soul-heavy stone.*

Sing, as to women you knew before me.
*So many gone.*

Ring for others who'll follow my shadow.
*Now but one.*

I lie among loss, and ruin, and glaciers.
*One torch, one cave.*

This is my answer to layers of sorrow.
*Ululate love.*

The sea snows.  The snow I scoop from waters—
*This one place.*

Melts on my palm.  Oh!  Love's weather!
*One mingled race*

# Yevgeny's music

**Longings of
the robot arm**

1.

The untuned may be in tune by chance, remain in tune,
a hand among starlings,
yet hard as a saucepan, or boinging like bedsprings,

lean and clean as a staple in a finger,
periodic as a pick, point-first on rock.

I might have been mush, a many-eyed potato
sunk in thickish loam,
or tumbling, wave-flung, ceaseless gravel,
or soursalt that sweetens a glass of tea.

Yet I must be Yevgeny, like a fork stabbing flank,
but gladder, gentler, more generously
desperate, slapping at my telos
among the smooth stones.

2.

O gullets craving knowledge, acid and bubble!
They desire cooked beet root, blood, baked apple.

How secret, aimless, is the life of the dying.

The sky's alight with jagged tendon
that no one sung or cast in wax.
Soon by night there is chanting at our backs.

Yet I want all my alloys to come alive
though they scream in every unoiled hinge,
though armor purples when ax hacks vein,
though all my silicon sizzles.

Can't my hand tear summer lutes by the strings?
Won't heaven sing through me as if my million holes
could strain out all clumsiness and longing—
in tune with the sun-trounced moon?

# Ball lightning

*God is day and night, winter and summer, war and peace, surfeit and hunger; but he takes various shapes, just as fire, when it is mingled with spices, is named according to the savor of each.*
*Heraclitus*

*This world, which is the same for all, no one of gods or men has made. But it always was, is, and will be an ever-living Fire, with measures of it kindling, and measures going out.*
*Heraclitus*

On Nevsky by the Dom Knigi renovation,
Taurus jeers at the titans on the deco dome top,
who muscle up a glassy globe
placed there by Singer Sewing Machine.

Below, cross-legged on pavement, a streetsinger
beats time on a head-shaped drum,
hollow, with a rounded tone.
Like the god's voice, but without the god.

Without even the demigod, the hemidemisemigod.
The bull-man, revved up, ready to explode—listens:
That rhythm?  Is it an empire falling?
Is that glass kniving into Nevsky tar?

The canal today blue and smooth as Iznik tile.
Heaven knows why this weary-looking man
has dropped a handline
into the globe's reflection,

rippling it.  The water settles, then explodes.
A carp flaps on the embankment
breathing air.  Everything's
waiting to be caught.  The god is here.

## Appearance from lightning strike on soil

**I. E. Gortunov (male), programmer, engineer. 14 years old, July 1952. Interview 1997. Daytime. Village, Enishevo of Smolenskaya oblast, Russia.**

**Boys and I were fishing. A black cloud approached and a thunderstorm began. We hid in the wooden building of a mill, in the pole basement. A bright flash broke out during strong rain and the broken trajectory of a linear lightning suddenly appeared. It struck into the body of the earthen dam. Simultaneously I felt a strong electric shock into my bare feet. In spite of this, I detected a blinding ball of the size of an orange fruit ascending into the air 20 m from me, originating from the place where the linear lightning struck. It was of red colour, like the colour of a ruby laser; and irradiated more intensely than an incandescent lamp of 200 W. Its clear-cut surface was well seen. The ball was hissing and slightly crackling. It got to a height of 3–4 m by flying over an arc in length about 10 m with a speed about 1 m s-1, descended to the ground, and exploded. Its sound was like a cannon shot. Totally, it lived for about 15 s. After the thunderstorm we investigated the place of the linear lightning strike, and found a crater of about 70 mm diameter and a corkscrew dip. We could not detect the place of the ball lightning explosion.**

There are grooves and dips on earth where the god walked.
Fruits of the god, and heats, and freezes.
Can the god be brought down into black ceramic?
Can the god be crazing on fired mud? Will he break
like a dam? Will ichor scour the mounds?

Tonight, even moths cannot sleep.
Their painted wings quake from too much flapping.
They land on sticky silk, and none go free.
In the arachnosphere, hopes belong to the spider.
The god is cobwebs on a vase, windtraps in the stratosphere.

The god in wait, and nothing can elude him.
In pursuit, and none will match his speed.
No, lovers, no one outflies the god.
Who else may bleed the earth, may trap the blood
in a brazier and cook it till it strikes like a snake?

Light shoots point to point across the soul,
and this bullet too is god.  Nets brush
in a network.  Hearts meet and tear—
like clay pounded together, pulled taut, they break.
Your breath catches in the back of my throat

like a hook.  It is your mortal breath,
the breath of circuses and war, but what is all
your violence to a god?  This is how he forms you,
geosphere, biosphere.  He beats you like clay.
You crackle.  The god is here.

### *Penetration through a windowpane, penetration into electric outlet*

**M. I. Oleneva (female) a pensioner. Observation 1955, a letter with description 1990. Reaction—fear. City, Kstovo near Nizhnii Novgorod, Russia.**

**It was gloomy before raining, but with no thunderstorm. My son, my mother and I were sitting by the table. The table was covered with an oilcloth. A small windowpane was opened by 100 mm. A fireball rolled through this space. It was very slightly yellow. We were all scared and did not move. A white electric outlet made of china was 0.5 m from us. The ball began to crawl inside this through one of the two holes. It almost all entered into the outlet, but the tail, the last part of the ball, was drawn into the other hole. Then a strong explosion was heard. A fire and a lot of soot appeared. The electric outlet was broken into pieces and its parts became black.**

Taurus' horned head begins to pulse.
Everywhere are hints of balls and spheres:
Camel humps, articulated shoulder,
semicircle moon, an almost round grave,
a woman's peaking breasts, arch of agitated cats,
a robin-pecked worm, balling up,
a robot at the bottom of the sphere of the world,
measuring a sphere of heat uprising.
Its lover robot, on a great circle plane, geolocates him.

On an ordinary day, the body celestial
electrifies the eye, floating music remembered,
banded planets, neutron stars.
Ping. Ping. They fire at our sensors,
perturbing magnets, straightening hair.

In what sphere is Taurus? Unpopulated light?
An endless, parched darkness, an intergalactic No?
He charges a market's open-air booths,
rips at a palace's red-berry bushes,
spits balls of foam at the bronze chizhik pyzhik.
They hit the bird's feet. They don't slide
into the river—will he have luck for a 1000 years?

A nightingale loses its song inside its beak.
Ravens claw at a round mole, shredding.
Treebuds open out from the center of all growing.
Fluff explodes in fusillades.
Horizons twist, wrench apart.

Soul crosses into soul, borders popping.
Every god, every demon, every being has a sphere,
every second, every animal breath of air.
In a glass, water has a spherical cap.

Drink, bull-man.  Ride the blue cloudspider.
Europa drinks from the same web of waters.
Bright balls burst.  The god is here.


*Swaying soap bubble that was broken into uneven pieces*

**V. N. Nezamaikin (male) a student engineer. 20 years old, the end of
June 1972. Interview 1992. Settlement Kopos, Ukraine.**

**In the morning I went hunting to a shore of the Dnieper river. The sky
was clean, with no thunderstorm or precipitation. I came to an open
place on the high shore of the Dnieper and noticed a luminescent
object 7 m from me in the reeds. It was a ball of 100 mm diameter,
of a bright blue colour. It radiated light like an incandescent lamp of
100–200 W. Its matter, dense in appearance, was swaying, also resem-
bling a soap bubble. The ball stayed motionless in the air, 600–700
mm above the grass. Not thinking for long, I made a shot into it
with my shotgun. The bullet consisted of lead pellets. The ball's size
increased by 1.5 times, and after that it decayed with a bang. It broke
into uneven pieces. They dissipated and then disappeared near the
surface of the water. The whole event lasted for 1–1.5 min.**

Struck, we see. Seeing, we shriek.  Shrieking, we root, blossom, die.
The thunderbolt steers all things.
Our messages shower and zip in the blankness.
The god in the cobwebs catches and gathers them.
And feeds on them where no one can come near.
O ghost-pulses, ghost-memories, absorbed forgettings.
Nothing left of us but song.  The god is here.

## *Cotton-wool structure, unfortunate case*

**V. A. Rantsev-Kartinov (male) PhD in physics. 5 years old, autumn, 20:00 h, 1944. Interview 2000. Number of observers: 8. Settlement, Kupino near Novosibirsk, Russia.**

**A rain ended. There was no thunderstorm. It was quiet with no wind, and hot and stuffy. I observed this event outdoors at a distance of 30 m from the object. A woman went out from the house to fan a flatiron. I noticed a glowing ball at a distance of 2–3 m from her. It resembled a cotton-wool ball of fist-size, 70–90 mm. When the woman put her hand with the flatiron behind her neck, the ball flew into the iron. Before this, the ball was moving after the iron. The observation time was 1–2 s.**

**The woman fell on the ground. People took her and buried her (head out) in the ground (the traditional treatment for lightning strike victims). After 0.5 h her face turned blue and she died.**

Somewhere in metal memory, a forest.
Taurus' minerals came from there,
copper, tin, arsenic the hardener.

The limping blacksmith melted them all
and poured red metal into a mold,
cooled it, filed it, hammered layers till it rang.

Took it to a hill to check its conductivity,
left it out in lightning.
It came into its own.  The current

seized it like a spider net,
but it came out stronger—
in free electrons, in flow like water, in heat

like an animal, in light like the boulevards,
in speed like the Metro, in waves like the Baltic,
in longing for women, in love

for Europa, in the vacuum of love,
pressure cooker love, the love
that mixes and turns the troposphere,

love that electrifies
the music of the spheres,
her innocent look when clouds

pass over—her sky-blue look
even as clouds pass—
Be it so. "The god is here."

### Woolen-type structure, burnt grass

**M. V. Lozovsky (male) a student. 8 years old, summer 1983–1984.
Interview 1994. Settlement Voronovo 40 km from Moscow, Russia.**

**It was at 17:00–17:30 h, and a strong thunderstorm broke out with
a rain shower. There was a strong wind with air temperature 22–23
.C. My grandmother and I were returning from the forest. Suddenly
we noticed a ball 200–220 mm in diameter in a round clearing 15 m
from us. It was rolling with a spiral trajectory. The ball was rotating,
touched the ground and made a movement for 50 mm. It resembled
a tangle of woollen threads, as if blue threads covered a warp of red
threads. The intensity of its radiation could be compared with an
incandescent lamp of 120 W. We were scared and quickly went away.
The next day we saw that the surface of the clearing was burnt out, so
that its colour became brown-black.**

The babushkasphere visits everyone by night.
It cleans the brainwebs with vinegar.  It brightens the brain like birch.
The brain must be strong for beauty.  This the grandmothers know.

Cherries fall.  Men and bulls brighten for Europa.
Europa brightens like birch.  Taurus thinks of nothing else.
He thinks only of cherries and her brightness.
He must squeeze her.  He must read by her light.
He must breathe the bubbles of her atmosphere.  The god is here.

*Several objects, appearance from nowhere, separation of one object into 6–7, decay into three shell-type pieces and several small pomegranate grain-like pieces*

**A. S. Timoshuk (male), associate professor in chemistry. 6 years old, April 1946. Interview 1990. City, Belaya Tserkov near Kiev, Ukraine.**

**It was 10:00–11:00 h in the morning at the end of April. It was the beginning of a thunderstorm: a thunderstorm cloud was approaching very quickly, and thunder broke out. A branching linear lightning shorted wires, going from a wooden telegraph pole to the other side of the street and over a broken branch of an old poplar. The distance between the objects and me was about 25 m.**

**At the moment of the shorting of the wires a yellow-green flash appeared near the upper insulator on the telegraph pole, resembling the intensity of a flash of electric welding. Inside of it grew a white ball about 150 mm in diameter. It slowly rolled over the inclined wire, increasing its velocity, changed to the colour of melted red metal, and during rotation provided many sparks. The ball was perceived as light in weight but not a hollow formation. At the lowest point of the wire it jumped to a lower wire 5 m from the pole. At the lowest point of this wire it fell down to the poplar branch, covering the distance of 0.5–0.8 m between them. At the moment of touching a strong crack sound was heard. The branch was broken and inclined. The ball decreased in size, but 6–7 balls of 40–60 mm diameter appeared, running over the branches. Then they expired simultaneously.**

Approximately 3 s later a new ball of 120 mm diameter appeared from 'nowhere'. The place of its origin was 1 m to the right of the place of formation of the first ball. It moved over the inclined thick branch, accelerating, smoothly and elastically jumping over any un-evenness. It decreased to 90–100 mm, spreading many sparks. Then it jumped onto the roadway, where it jumped in a similar fashion to a gas balloon. The heights of its jumps were 200, 120 and 50 mm; in so doing the amplitudes decreased, but the frequency of jumps increased. Then the ball decayed into three big pieces of a shell shape and several further smaller pieces. The collection resembled a broken pomegranate with red grains on the ground. The destruction of the ball was viscous, similar to snow rolled-up into a snowball, whose structure is laminated. Parts disappeared non-simultaneously. Total duration of the event was 18–20 s.

So many spheres: Alpha-beta rains from a radium strip,
microballoons in radiation-slurping slurry,
a fist severed from its arm in a museum of curiosities,
the magnetosphere's Antarctic fluxion.
The god floating down from the deosphere,
balls of Uranus in the sea and Aphrodite,
the amorosphere with its transports, its landings
on a gravelly runway over permafrost melting,
on a stage in an opera where the sound of Italian
reminds the audience of falling water, and everyone leaves just dead.

Round emergences, curved convergences,
gradual bend of longitude and latitude,
right ascension, declination, in celestial navigation,
the telosphere to which all actions tend,
the dynosphere through which all movements arc,
the arcosphere in which all space
is a row of Soviet-style dwellings
before the solo volcanos of Petropavlovsk,
and whole armies of grandmothers come to market
with vats of round pink salmon eggs more plentiful than stars.

The dumposphere overfilled with garbage of the oblasts,
the credosphere of gullible tendencies,
the terpsichosphere where everyone dances with the god.
All wave arms, lock hands, hear trains.
Tie-rhythm, wheel-beat, humming near.
Out of nowhere, the god is here.

### Appearance from nowhere, large size, soft bubble, interaction with observers

**T. S. Sychevskaya (female) a teacher of pre-school. 17 years old, 20:00 h, June 1971. Interview 1998. 5 observers. City, Zapadnaya Dvina, Russia.**

In the evening my friends and I went to a dance. It was rather cool after a thunderstorm, but with no wind. We crossed the Moscow–Riga railway. We just had crossed the rails and suddenly noticed a spherical ball lightning over our heads. It was of 700–800 mm diameter. It appeared as if from nowhere. We got frightened, squatted, and connected our hands, creating a circle. The ball suddenly began to move over us in a circle, and it also moved up and down. It was at a height of 0.5 m above the ground. Then it 'chose' my head and began to jump on it, up and down, like a ball. It made more than 20 jumps. It was as soft as a bubble and I did not even feel its weight. I felt cold from it. The ball resembled a gel of white-grey colour. Its boundary was like a soap bubble. Its glow could be compared with that of an incandescent lamp of 200 W. Inside the ball (at 1/3 of its diameter) the glow was more intense than outside. Then it ascended and disappeared unexpectedly. After this contact we were throwing up.

Sphere of the individual, everyone unique,
the collectivity—uniqueness in all,
sphere nichovo ne znayu, where nothing is known,
BBs in Kalashnikov BB rifles,
a golf ball a cosmonaut drove into orbit,
the spheres of grease in sorrel soup,

concentric spheres of an infinite regression
to ever-smaller personal divisions.
Taurus in a sphere of uncontrolled creation,
his head in poplar tangles bobbing on a windless day,
a garble of spherical poplar seed planets.
In what sphere is Europa with her elegance and ease?
Will poplars reach the roundness
of her eyes?  Will they touch her tongue,
change all to one?  The god is here.

Vibrating gel, thinness of the sacred—
anyone can break it with a spit or a sigh.
Awake, we see only death. In slumber, only sleep.
But for a moment, the sea may be clear as it is deep.
Curve of the return when no line goes there,
return of the curve where only lines had been,
interconnection—orbits, braincanals,
gravitic tunnels from Earth to Mars or Venus,
gods in a tree, goddesses in mushrooms.
Fluff skims a river.  Something bursts.
Sound floats across the brain like a distant ship.
It runs like golden rain through the temporal lobe,
triggers a glimpse of Love, smell of sliced pear,
unannounced, a heaven.  The god is there.

Radiant, love in circumnavigations,
circumlocutions, circumambulations.

There is a thunderstorm. No thunderstorm.
Tree.  Or none.

Love's a ball.
We're balancing bears.  Someone 's

always about to fall.
The rain is always

raining till it's done,
until it rains again.

A bounce like a plectrum
across the branches.

In each moment, a Europa
or an ending.

Something bursts.
The god is here.

# Messages from the god

### 1. Dei/logue

**The god inhabiting the bull-gargoyle practices speeches to Europa as the bull listens.**

The god will not shut up:
"History ends in piles and husks.
Storms white, storms black, earth gone.

Everywhere, earth is gone.
Railroads arrow from the steppe's end through far villages.
Men throttle chickens, trample fields,

trade bombs for apples, and apples for bombs.
as if some other earth—a green-bottle eye—
will rise over the taiga.

But there is no such earth.  We inherited no other.
Black wave, black wave breaking with a white,
exhaustions of soot and snow.

Our design is—things run out.
Thus the steppe scrub hunkers low,
and sleepy sheep mill in spirals, converging.

What's more unmoored than a droop-eyed god?
Tired from too much sleeping, I would like
a nap.  On goose down cushion,

to count waves on a lake, from a cloud room
to glide over warrior nicks and hacks,
and to dream from the beginning

through the slow monotonies of the ticking world,
till my dream comes to you,
my sweet sweet you,

as if you were the first and brightest ray of moon
to play green-stalk lyres
in budded fields.

Light is the purest antidote to woe,
cutting through grain,
spewing from a girl.

Even to a god who snorts and snores,
the light is warm.  It strikes the ore of shadows,
and even a god is warmed."

## 2. Bull/china

**The bull-gargoyle's
reaction to the god's
rehearsal**.

The warm ax-head voice
hits Taurus behind the eyes, drowsying the bull.
Horns drop into a bowl,

splattering an archipelago of sour cream
halfway to Finland
or just blebbing the warped linoleum

as coffee steams up from his espresso cup
in a mocking cloud, like a mock-up of the god,
fogging the basement café

where card tables
lurch out of kilter
when touched by a fork or news—

as if gravity were constantly lumping, shifting,
in the changing magnetics
of kettle and plate,

unsettled by divine agitations—
The god zeroed on the girl, the multiplying zeros
bleb upon bleb almost reaching her.

Taurus twitches
in a coffee-breeze.
The china rocks as he moos.


### 3. Distance

**The god tries out another speech to Europa; distinctions between human and god.**

"Europa, my apple, look at your kind.
Every cell breaks, or wears to little heaps.
All of your waters rush out, pooling,

all of your pools go cement-gray and steam
in shavings, urine, swampgas, wind.
Man's a heap of cells who fires little lightnings,

But the greater lightning accumulates in gods
who beautify or foul, as case may be,
rainwater, floodwater, salt-sweat sea

with electric muscularity.
We shock the sceptre from an emperor's hand
and prod some child to use it for a bludgeon

It needles through blue beads,
to add another necklace to the empire—till we tire
and ocean salts the sceptre.

Wars go on in the aftermath of war
as a flood piles wave over wave on barren rock.
Sad earth, sorry earth, drools and bawls.

Her ancient skin chafes like the skin of a newborn,
tongue-tied and toothless, in a shroud of cloud.
These aren't our wars, nor she our mother.

Our battles rage beyond bliss or erosion.
We roam radiant banks of sun-bloody bays
and scheme for our hybrids and concubines.

Immortality alone betrays us.  We never lie down
in the green stalk land, nor skip stones,
nor yield to moon-scarred flows.

And therefore I crave the mortal gush.
In a breathing hide, I charm you in a pasture
till puffballs blacken the summer soil."

### 4. Block out

**An interrupted
reverie**

Staring down the coffee's black,
the bull drops into his own thoughts.
Dandelions yellow the sad little lawn on a concrete island.

They send olfactory contrails
that brush him with desire
cut by crankcase oil and smoke.

"The god's not entering my thoughts at all," thinks Taurus,
thrilled in a dream of crossing—
at a canter to dare buses to dent him.

Down he'll bend and smear nose with pollen.
Taut lips will yank sweet plants by the roots
and toss them, and catch.

Tongue will indulge in a mash of prickly leaves,
a pleasure he normally shuns
in the presence of a girl or god.

The god! The shouting, headlong as a train—
*Europa, Europa*, how much *Europa*! The bull
waves down the waitress for his check.

## 5. Among the mortals

The god encourages
Europa to see herself
as chosen.

"O earth, domain of wet-haired men
whose walkways are cracking, whose foundations craze.
Fates faultline through their days.

But in the end, one. I say, 'Die,' and they do.
If I say so or not, they die, in fact.
Like dandelions, newts, the blind rosy moles.

Did we promise more
than a nailscratch in clay
the summer rain would smooth away?

Or that their lyres and combs
would hang like butterflies in velvet,
or we'd make mementos

of their falling flesh,
in swan, seamonster, snakes, a girl,
mere outline, yet flint for memory?

A few we favor. We assume a form,
no longer zing about, but breathe,
shed the awesome shapelessness of power,

and hay pokes us. We shake off dew
as moonlight needles through leaves of an oak.
For a second, every air is new:

the barred owl's barking so the fieldmice quake,
an army lazing by aspens, basking in flares,
half-dead and half-awake.

And we spume a chosen mortal
like a gale across a lake
that had only heard of gales from veering seabirds."

### 6. Intercourse

**The god rehearses how he will implore Europa to approach.**

"Be water to my wind.  Come, reddened as a flare.
Bring earth's charms
to the cloud-curtained god

till dead sun burns up golden doves,
and seasalt cures the boiled egg soul.
Bring timeless gasps till you grow cold, and I go on.

Till you're calm, though sky's an inkblot,
though Heaven is noise,
and human and god still dream of each other

traveling tracks through barely touching trees.
A railway shoots.  A city falls toward dawn.
The sediment thickens, more perfect for dreams.

And I dream of you, my apple, my pulsar.
O, blue-shifting whistle,
bring light back to me."

### 7. Temples

**Taurus's headache. the pharmacy; his own thoughts of Europa**

The god is a threnody in Taurus's brainpan.
On the stage-set of his brainpan,
the god has the lines.

How does His Antiquity hope to win her?
By train wheels
wheezing more rust than steel?

Taurus pounds the concrete
from café to pharmacy.
The cashier line undulates through the store

and back to beginning—head-eating-tail.
At the booth he asks for aspirin
"and something to keep me awake."

His insides already coffee bean lava.
Head about to hatch
into a million copper worms,

to link with the deepest bottom of some White Sea.
He likes to peer down dark
to see if darkness looks back.

So today, all he discerns of Europa
are the green-black feathers of the greener depths
where odd life dangles bulbs.  His questing eyes

touch a ring of tentacles in muted light.
The soft-mouthed sea flower gulps—eyes gone. . . .
The pharmacist, looking at him quizzically,

has arrayed the bull's relief
in a pyramid of boxes and vials, receipt on top,
like an altar for knife and animal.

## 8. Fertilizer

**The god shifts to a monologue on his own mortality; a storehouse of discarded gods; thoughts of fertility.**

"Forgotten before I was banned— a congeries of marble
in a dank museum basement, arm touching leg.
You could not tell my brother's nose

from my crumbling thumb.
Then within four small walls,
a thousand gods more were dumped into the pile,

and those who did the dumping
were dumped on our backs, decades of clatter and shatter.
Ice crystals in winter.  Window sweat in summer.

A weed or two grew like liberation from the floor,
cracked cement shaken by tanks and artillery.
The mounting count of gods

from every flat space of the realm,
from every tall mountain and windy plateau,
from tribes of desultory sheep

that had split off from the herd
and made temples of tufts and tumuli.
Fleece gods, then, and toothed and hooved,

who had taught games of chance
to any who would listen, but now—
pricked with pentothal through the tongue,

could only say, "We won't last a week or two."
What crops could grow in powdery marble?
Cellars, dismal rooms, the rage that burns them,

that smell of burning hair and starving skin.
Jaws and hips of children pulverized in factories,
painted into houses, smeared by mimes.

All beside the point, the fate of bulls, men, or gods:
Whom to strike down?
Whom to save?

All beside the point.  Only water, loam, and bone,
sperm filling the fracture lines of clay—
seed craving holy sun."

### 9. Such gifts

**Taurus lurches out
into the city.**

A forsaken park. The bull-man pauses to breathe.
As a white flock ravages a tiny patch of grass,
Taurus can already smell the river.

He smells waterbugs and gnats.
whose careless tracks
leave scarcely a ripple where currents roll.

He too feels hardshelled, barely noticed
trudging tank-like through St. Petersburg,
past sputtering carburetors, Vespas and Planetas,

Taurus—"driver" to the talking fireball,
who rattles and wheedles
and hoots for Europa.

### 10. Ochi chernya

**The god desires
Europa's dark,
mortal eyes.**

"So many armies, so many icy floors.
The boot-ground wheat grains
loll in muck.

Leather torn from a horse
ties a shoulder to an arm.
The glorious resourcefulness

of humans as they fall
with every face of bliss or oblivion!
Earthworms

vacuum their blackened eyes,
widening the pupils
like pots dug out for seed.

And you, my darling, leaf and stem,
thornapple, come
and grow in my sight,

grow fanatic
in my breath,
fill the flowerpots with light."

### 11. Peter's walk

**Out in the city, near Hare Island, the bull-gargoyle thinks of a myth of the city's founding, multiplicity.**

Flowerpots!  The bull begins to shuffle
past a palace door framed by spindly roses—
wan, sparse leaves on the stem.

The pots have a firebird glazed into the clay
that seems about to fly away, faded as brown
as the waning blooms.

The scent sends Taurus on a rotten sweet drunk.
He senses the peat on top of the pots,
like the island peat that Peter cut

and laid crosswise: *The city will be here.*
On a day he wasn't there, so Taurus is thinking.
Isn't history a day someone was there,

and not mere fluff that rides on air, scintillating everywhere
when the night comes fast as a sheet pulled taut
and snapped across your memory?

You stand in the street, watch the pied petals fall
out of time, or can't recall
what story you were telling in what habitation.

Droplets pull new smells from soil,
the smell of must, of rock and roll,
glass up the nose, black tobacco,

chemical reels of yellowed films moldering in official rooms
no one thinks to open.  Eternal friction
brings you to yourself, dragging along a street

where once you hid your face, and now you walk
smelling attars of rain, bull nose tickled by fennel and fires
that burn in industrial memory.

And in the midst of all the snares and frauds,
the drowning thunder of the exasperating god,
it may be true:  the city will be here, framing you
    against a wall.

Perhaps a woman's finger on the shutter
will flash the darkness, catch the bull
about to go full-tilt across a square

because the god is with you,
because you've never been so much yourself—
seen in a shop window,

doubled and redoubled,
or like a hologram, *en plein aire*,
because the god is all desiring, yet gives all.

## 12. Capercaillie cock

**The god implores
Europa through a
country dream.**

You dream at the surface.  Land meeting river.
Light meeting impenetrable river,
but only near the surface; only there.

Sedge and cranberries are bobbing up.
Shuffles of birch bark and bubbles touch the light.
Rock-torn marten fur floats in glare.

In your eyes, for long seconds, the surface is alive.
In your ears, for long seconds, you hear the capercaillie,
deaf to the world when it sings to its mate.

Only then can it be killed, when its song is all,
red-browed and fantailed, too stiff to fly.
Beak to the sky, the cock sings for your light.

From the boat of your dreams, Europa,
hear the capercaillie, tune surfacing,
submerging, resurfacing, till night.

### 13. Genealogy

**The god practices explaining himself to Europa; his origins; his manifestations.**

It is a bad night.  The god blabs on and on.
Lightning rages over the Neva.
Taurus notices a door in a Rostral Column

where no opening has been before.
He pulls the door.  A stairway shimmers.
Now up and up the looming stairs,

trying to get the god out of his head.
"When my father tried to eat me,
mother fed him stone.  For my name was stone,

and she hid me in mud.  In the mud of great rivers,
she hid me in coffins
that floated downriver when ice broke in spring.

And I rose against him from the many-armed mud.
I killed him again and again."
Taurus moves one booted hoof, then the next.

Water rushing, rising up the column,
now at his ankles, now his knees.
"Therefore, I have only *more* to give—

frost around the moon, the innerness of trees,
over and over of dawning day,
obscuring air that twinkles a star

again and again and again.
I'm storm—repeats of shocks, winds, drops.
rattles of barrels in the heavens.

I'm time that feeds the flood,
and nothing is enough, and I give more and more,
and still there's more to give—

to bathe a waning earth, her cities winking out,
to pole a load of souls across a river of stars
to banks where they'll wait to be born."

### 14. Flood/light

**The flood whirls the god; he looks for Europa.**

Taurus from a high step watches as the flood
rips the city's foundations.
Khruschev-era walls collapse, plow into a church.

The canals are thick with junk—scaffolding, paintcans,
a sculpted sunburst light of the divine,
a coconut painted with the face of Peter,

gilt replicas of Petersburg public art
from the era of Catherine to the Soviets' fall
swirling by the souvenir stalls.

"I whirl, spiral like a poplar seed,
linger like a poplar seed, sprout among piles.
I'm straining upward.  Love confounds me.

Is that surface?
Is it sky?
Bring your light."

### 15. Coda

Light comes in a breath,
and then gone,
thinks the bull.

Light dreams
in a breath, and it's
dream, dreams the god.

Light sings in
a breath, one
song, moos the girl.

The rain-cracked moon
pressed into a ball—for one
blink, whole.

## DVD from Europa

**The bull-gargoyle receives an animated message from Europa; a version of a Russian fairy tale.**

Europa, in translucent fabrics, embraces a bull-man.
She in tears, his eyes ravines.
He must go and says in his rumbling way:
do not leave the apartment, or heed evil words.

She checks her messages every day.
She has many correspondents.
Every day she writes of love.

Old Woman sends a message.  Who is Old Woman?
"A walk in this garden will ease your grief."

Old Woman is so right.  A walk
in a garden.  Old Woman
has sent a virtual garden.
The ferns are tall.  The flowers
have shapes of lion and fox.

Out goes Europa, strolls through the flowers.
A spring-fed pool extends clear, cool hands.
They hold a message:  "Come in, come in."

Off slips her gown.  She walks into the water.
Suddenly an old woman strikes her on the neck.

Europa, changed, is a white duck,
and the witch is now Europa, trying on her robe,
painting Europa's face on her own.
When the bull-man comes home, he does not know.

The white duck lays eggs in high, cold reeds.
Three hatchlings go exploring.
They stray near the apartment.
The false Europa knows them by their smell.

She turns on a burner.
Gas dizzies the chicks.
With the hard hand of a corpse
the crone beats and kills them all.

When the white duck finds her babies
(kerchief-white, minnow-cold),
she holds them with her wings and laments
in a voice that is almost Europa's.

Hearing, the bull-man chases after her in vain,
then finds the needed words:
"Birch behind, girl before."

Now a birch tree stands behind him, Europa before.
A magpie flies with seedpods
holding waters of life, of speech.
The waters pour.  Chick skin shudders.
More waters pour, and the babies
tell the Old Woman's misdeeds.

Tied to a cloud, she's dragged by one leg.
Her logic goes barren as crow-ravaged corn.
Her cells fly off like hawk-hunted sparrows.

Finally, Europa, white-winged in woman's body,
and her feathered babies lift off.
They fly around the bull-man,
crying joy in ducky tongues,
their call still roughened
by the high, cold reeds.

The tableau ends.  The screen blanks to silhouettes—
ducks like arrows—and
*From your white duck, Europa.*

# Vapors: dawn

### 1.    Ur-cloud

The bull-gargoyle's message to the model Europa; to meet her in St. Petersburg under the constellation Taurus during White Nights.

In the all ever-seething, don't we all seethe as one?
Since all started as one, don't I feel you
quicken, even a continent away?

Steam boils out of star-born kettles.
It might be mousebreath or ghostliness of manholes,
might be a bombsplash, or ancient lace

conjured on a humid stroll
by grayed-out city waters,
by the Church Over Spilled Blood.

### 2.    Far away near

And so, my darling, I look for you
here, on the far side of time,
on my Russian streetcorner.

Not knowing where you are, I look up at night,
the just-past-dusk that passes for darkness,
where the dead meet mainly the dead.

Not knowing, I scan screens—
bull-faced, bull-intentioned—
breathing mainly delirium.

### 3.    Anyone, anywhere

I'll meet you anywhere elements are forming,
any year by a skin-chewing sky,
where beacons gore the scintillating dark,

and sleepers follow lights as if led by a god,
only to wake in bric a brac—
foundered memories, bladed moons.

We'll meet where anyone met before,
we who were nothing but wounds before,
aches in astringent waves.

Come, love, we'll flop in all the rainbows.
The sun passing through us
will tell what's to be.


**4.      Once in Tyre**

Remember, near Tyre, l came to you.
Though all the mist-crazed girls stopped to gape,
I was calm and warm and slow.

You ran fingers down my flank as down a map—
finding outlines of battlements, and shady arcades
in a ruin the gods had scarred there,

and bodies fractured, fallen on rocks,
before bulls knew pens or gods had names.
Moist and barefoot on a ledge, you traced my hide.

I thrust my head into wet brush,
pulled out hanks of heal-all.
You trembled like wind across a pool.


**5.      Signs**

Now cellphone billboards everywhere
beam that we're no longer creatures
of the earth, and so I look for you in canals,

among caryatids and statues,
on the back of gold-winged gryphons
whose mouths hold up the footbridge. . .

What beauty could be more tempting
than the hazy slipper of the Pleiades,
barely glinting in your sign?

Let our signs join.  A bull can deliver
hoof sparks, hot breath, tongue huge as a god's,
a rod that can shiver seas.

## 6.    Healed

A herd of ambulances, crossing Fontanka,
splatters iron hides of the bridge's black steeds.
They glisten with the pathos of eternal stars

that gleam for the angry pleasure of gleaming,
when keyboards are a rage of rain.
Do wounds ever join?  Geography is pain.

There's a scratch on your city the shape of a bay.
Mine has a bulge like Mercury,
Let's out-heal any miracle before,

you there, and I here, and a rained-over moon
and vans reviving their deliveries.
Then we'll climb from one red ocean, out of time.

# Bakery

## 1.

**Europa imagines
the bull-gargoyle will
abandon her, and
she'll work in
a bakery.**

All that was— veins without the leaf,
crust and crumb scorched black,
courtyard soot and frost and soot.

Look! A million birds in the apple tree.
They've no interest in bread.
They puncture tiny apples.

I sweep the punctured skins. I sing a punctured song.
Why do I slump,
folded over, and cold?

## 2.

**She addresses the
bull-gargoyle; her
dreams.**

Perhaps, beast, you did not know old women dream,
and truth gave bone to dreams
long before I dreamt of you.

Did you drain my every fate
except to wait, except to wait,
and sweep the waiting into piles

and tip the waiting down a can
and stir it in the can with rain
until it's time to wait again?

No. I watch the bakery's TV.
I look for lightning on the maps, and hatless rush outside
and try to drink you down.

To catch you on my tongue
and swig you till you're gone. Then bolts move past.
No droplet drums. Alone,

92

I moan into my washing pail.
Breath makes patterns, rise and fall,
in suds and apple scums.

3.

**She recalls the**
**bull-gargoyle.**

I was from everywhere, from nowhere, sought by all,
and when the bull approached,
from searing dusk,

awesome as a vessel transported from a temple,
I (who believed most
in phosphorous, in matches—

the blue, the snap, the risk of extinction,
the cigarettes that kept me thin,
buds unfurling orange, the book erupting)

I lit like holy oil, and everywhere
went bright,
even smoke from his heaving sides.

4.

**Their lights**
**intermingling**

Then I was on a hill facing a bull,
naked and near
and I almost fainted.

Lamps—girl and bull—
rays interlaced like hands,
a lattice nothing could break,

though the day was black-sleek
and sky was a flash
hitting vessels and humors,

among minerals and smog,
only I and you
and the horizons.

5.

**Europa's present**

Now the bonds of my molecules fray and give way,
and you do nothing, bull,
harrower, discarder.

though I sweep through apples, wrappers, crusts,
breaks in this bakery's knobby breads,
apple pirozhki tender in the center,

as I was once,
now a bug broomed
in char from an oven,

faithful today as a bug to her god,
as god to his scatterings, as you to Europa,
faithful as I to my broom.

6.

**Her mind jittery as a
flour beetle**.

My thoughts blow like flour over flour
erasing the footsteps
of *tribolium confusum*.

I can hardly remember the glint of your neck
when I leaned to kiss your back and felt my depths
roll across your hide.

I can keep track of nothing now.
I forget why this baker's teasing
torments me,

smiling in malice or pity as I stumble,
expression fuzzy though five feet away
while I rest on a garbage can,

boots gonging
under a shifting, brownish
cloud of starlings.

7.

**Recalling their union**  You sounded like that gong
against my knuckles,
bovine heaver, bulbous twitcher,

when I pounded you from below,
your bulk suspended
as if the heat of Furnace Earth held it fixed there

while I shouted—
I can't remember if in pain or pleasure—
that a creature so cumbrous

could be cajoled to ring
by soft fists' battering
like rain on a dome,

like fruit swinging ravaged
by songbird beaks,
the interruptions of wings.

8.

Where are you now?
**She imagines him**  Do you lean from a cantilevered roof,
**now**.  as if about to somersault off and chase a wren?

Or crouch in a niche
above a gold-green door,
horns poking curved beyond your shoulders?

The lean that leaned me,
horns that curved me,
to adore your force and ceremony?

You do not visit now.
You've hurled me down like bent coins
bearing the trenched face

of an exiled concubine,
who used to sway through
the very thresholds

where you perched high, an unblinking guardian.
Had a prince seen you blinking,
would he have let you in?

9.

**His horns**

I let you in.  A girl-flower let you in.
A meadowsweet ablush at things
that humans do to bulls,

heedless that your horns were milled for goring.
In the end, we were horn-mad.
You struck wall.  Struck heart,

my mortar giving in.
Your horns abrading red sparks.
Till red went dark.

10.

**Words find her**

When you bellow, the churches and motorcycles
tremble.  Europa's voice has never
moved a hair on any head.

Yet words come to me like starlings.
One by one beaks pierce red bubbles;
one by one, they swallow tear-shaped seeds

on afternoons when I pull every gown from every drawer
and try them out, and flush because they fit,
because I'm even smaller than I was before,

and I dazzle the lightbulbs, and pirouette,
mouth witticisms and almost-prayers
for the nuzzlings of a gem-horned beast.

11.

**In his absence**

Why, bull, have you left me now to live or die,
guideless through mists and quarries,
groping for a boundary?

I am shapeless and black.
On every street, I wear your shadow.
My dust blows over concrete like a million birds.

Won't you pity your little cloud of disarrays?
Won't you charge me through a decrepit doorway
splashing in a sluice of apples?

You have partaken.
You have tossed away.
I arch back my neck

and look for you zeroing down at my soul,
small as a seed, small as a crumb,
your glassy gaze upon my song of ashes.

# Borealis

### City

**The bull to Europa**

The god once built a city in my heart.
Or who else drained the starry, swampy brine?
Who hammered down the pylons of long pine?
The landfills and the lanes were soaked and bright.
Armloads of dung, a pecker's ratatat.
Now I'm sleepless in a lightning-withered night.
Wind reeks of gasoline and too much talk,
of whacks wedged into necks.  I hump my back
and run at every net until I'm caught.
Is it rain will slaughter me or blessed luck?
If god's left hand once pistoned on my snout,
I still wait for his right.  Mapless, I walk
on a shattered arch in reedy riverlands.
Let sands break sandhills down to smaller sands.

### Wind-flowers: *anemone coronaria*

Let sands break sandhills down to smaller sands.
If I dig my knees a pit, the sand is sky.
Beige moonlit motes are spinning off my hands,
and now's a hot glass bubble in my eye
bending these hours into a honied lump—
kasha, nasturtiums, clover, gritty oats,
fermented hay that reeks midsummer damp.
There's moistened breath, and sand, and
    hard-hooved fits.
Here's kale and sand, and sand and honeysuckles.
And now the god, a hurricane of sand,
outscreaming sparrow flocks and barn-eave swallows,
hoists up my spinning soul.  Old rasp, old wind,
may dragonflies and teeming ants come fling
anemones down to my reckoning.

## Between

Anemones down to my reckoning;
vine-darkened, speckled roses; monk's hood leaves;
bog star collapsed in heaps.  Can some bright wing
sweep down between our skull-sacks and the waves
of crawling shade?  Between the clouds' brim and
the mole rat's murk, here's half a light-filled inch—
low pasture weeds, my spiky boulder-land.
I wedge an eye in there.  I crunch the crunch
of sheaves in side to side work of a jaw.
Who knows if the work is mine or from the blue?
One raven's talon jabs another's caw.
You shout.  I duck.  You duck.  I shout: *It's you?*
There's half an inch to shout in and to see
a god's long tendrils joining you to me.


## Herd

A god's long tendrils joining you to me
drive green and knobby through the stockyard clay,
a mush roughened with sand and cell debris.
Why in god's grasp are so many thrown so low
a lintel beam seems distant as a star?
Earth rumbles phlegm.  Green guts reverberate.
The gates are latched, or there never was a gate.
A blade's behind the chute behind the door.
But praise the blade.  The god has joined us here
by our gazes, by the feet, upright or beast.
Beginning to beginning, we draw near,
never more near than at the darker last.
This blur-dark god was brighter than a bomb
in our closed eyes when they slid out of the womb.

## Mist

In our closed eyes, when they slid out of the womb,
already we agreed on names of clouds.
God's flock of terns was tearing at a loom.
God's cloth of vapor lay draped on the reeds.
Warehouse facades were pressing out like hulls,
when you, my cloud girl, crossing slippery stones,
and I, a bullock trotting among bulls,
both heard the bursts in seaside power lines.
The hours had fallen out of all the works,
the gears gone gap-toothed in their trains.
A few sleepers queued for loaves and small sardines.
You hurried off. A shower startled larks.
Drops tickled them to pipe and print the shore.
Then east dissolved. That first light flared no more.


## Aurora

Then east dissolved. That first light flared no more.
Dissolves and flares are all that we deserve
who hide from lightning when it slants
    toward shore.
If I forage the dense taiga, soon I starve.
But seized by a god, I leap along the steeps,
guzzle at wellsprings, chop the thin, cool grasses.
Hide white, and whiter than the airless tops,
I bull-dance down the scree. A woman pauses.
I know your shape, like ballads on the bone.
Your lips are ships that venture cruel sea
at the perfect speed, and on the perfect line
to venerate the god and vanquish me.
The sun-wind's curtain twists the dark past dawn—
your glance a warming, gaze aurora-green.

## Archaeology

Your glance a warming, gaze aurora-green
across my farm-wild hair, across the bindings
and the leaves, across the hard, half-rotten sheen
of leather thumbed through chapters, past all endings.
One *Ah* begets a flood, the flood a spin
of sheetrock's give and jostled bedsprings' bark.
Lightnings will smelt the past.  Yet you've begun
your beautiful time, and I've brought you an arc,
a clasp to close.  I'm hammering it now—
though grasshoppers all die without a name,
a northern frost browns beet-greens down the row,
and I am old as bronze, whiter than lime.
Let this diadem be yours, let digging start.
The god once built a city in my heart.

## NOTES

Ball lightning reports in "Ball Lightning" were adapted from Abrahamson, Bychkov & Bychkov, "Recently Reported Sightings of Ball Lightning," *Phil. Trans. R. Soc. Lond.* A (2002) 360, 11–35.

"DVD from Europa" was adapted from A.N. Afanasyev, *Russian Fairy Tales*.

## ACKNOWLEDGEMENTS

*Arion:*               Ball lightning, Messages from the god,

*Blackbird:*           Attachment: Virtual matryoschka, Dream over
                       dream, Foreword, from The Scrapbook of Yevgeny
                       the Robot Arm

*Fulcrum:*             The gargoyle's entreaty

*Horizon Review:*     Europa's crossing, Visitation

*Pequod:*              Bakery, Houdini, It Would Be Better

*TriQuarterly:*        In the Beautiful City

*A Face to Meet
the Faces: An
Anthology of
Contemporary
Persona Poetry:*      To the stockyard bulls